Design: Jill Coote
Recipe Photography: Peter Barry
Recipe styling: Jacqueline Bellefontaine, Siân Davies,
Bridgeen Deery and Wendy Devenish
Jacket and Illustration Artwork: Jane Winton,
courtesy of Bernard Thornton Artists, London
Editorial: Laura Potts

CLB 3355
Published by Grange Books,
an imprint of Grange Books Limited,
The Grange, Grange Yard, London.
© 1993 CLB Publishing,
Godalming, Surrey, England.
All rights reserved.
Printed and bound in Singapore
Published 1993
ISBN 1-85627-314-8

# THE LITTLE BOOK ·OF·

# *Pasta*

## RECIPES

*A compact, easy-to-follow guide to creating perfect pasta dishes.*

*Grange*
BOOKS

# Introduction

*T*he basic recipe for pasta – which at its most simple is literally a *paste* made from flour and water – appears in many cuisines, and takes many forms. It is, however, particularly associated with the Italian and Chinese culinary traditions. The debate as to which of these nations should be credited with its invention has been hotly argued. One thing, however, is certain. Though not unique to Italian cooking, pasta has to a certain extent become synonymous with it.

Pasta comes in a bewildering variety of shapes and sizes. The fundamental reason for this profusion does not lie, as many would believe, in Italian extravagance, or in rivalry between competing dried pasta manufacturers. In fact, different varieties of pasta absorb different amounts of sauce, with some shapes of pasta complementing some sauces better than others. For example, long varieties of dried pasta are best served with oil-based sauces, and generally speaking do not combine well with meat sauces. Rich, creamy sauces and meat sauces, on the other hand, go well with short-cut varieties of pasta, especially those which are hollow, or have grooves where the sauce can be trapped.

Most supermarkets now stock a wide variety of fresh, as well as dried pasta. Many people prefer dried pasta, for the simple reason that they are more familiar with it and know exactly how to cook it. Like dried pasta, fresh pasta is cooked in boiling salted water, with a little oil to stop it sticking together. Cooking times for fresh and

dried pasta vary, with dried pasta taking slightly longer. It is essential that pasta is not over-cooked, as there is nothing less appetizing than a plateful of limp, soggy spaghetti or tagliatelle. Pasta should be cooked until it is *al dente*, which means tender but firm. There are many ways to test whether pasta is cooked, but the best way is to take a piece and taste it.

Pasta sauces do not have to be elaborate. In fact some of tastiest, most-loved sauces can be prepared very quickly. Melted butter, black pepper and the lightest sprinkling of freshly grated Parmesan cheese, for example, or the classic *carbonara* sauce with cream, eggs and bacon make delicious easy sauces. The essence of a good pasta sauce lies in the use of fresh ingredients, whose flavours enhance each other. Ripe tomatoes, fragrant herbs, black olives and juicy, sweet peppers, are commonly found in pasta sauces.

This book is an invaluable companion to the experienced and inexperienced cook alike. The selection of recipes reflects the versatility of pasta, offering a range of recipes, from those that can be put together very quickly, such as *Tagliatelle with Garlic and Oil*, to the more elaborate baked dishes such as *Lasagne* and *Cannelloni*. The step-by-step instructions explain how to create a variety of perfect pasta dishes, highlighting the skills needed to make fresh pasta, and giving ideas for different fillings and sauces.

# Minestra

*SERVES 4-6*

*A wholesome soup which makes an ideal starter.*

PREPARATION: 15 mins
COOKING: 45 mins

115g/4oz short-cut macaroni
30ml/2 tbsps olive oil
1 onion
1 carrot
1 stick celery
1½ litres/3 pints water
225g/8oz fresh spinach
2 tomatoes
1 tsp rosemary
2 tbsps chopped parsley
2 cloves garlic, crushed
60g/2oz Parmesan cheese, grated
Salt and pepper

**Step 1** Cut onion, carrot and celery into thick matchstick strips.

**Step 4** Add the shredded spinach leaves to the soup.

**1.** Cut onion, carrot and celery into thick matchstick strips.

**2.** Heat oil in a large, heavy pan, and fry vegetable strips until just browning, stirring occasionally.

**3.** Pour on water, add salt and pepper, and let simmer for 20 minutes.

**4.** Meanwhile, wash and cut spinach leaves into shreds, add to soup and cook for 10 minutes.

**5.** Scald and skin tomatoes, and chop roughly, removing seeds.

**6.** Add tomatoes, macaroni, garlic, parsley and rosemary to the soup, and simmer for a further 10 minutes.

**7.** Adjust seasoning. Serve with grated Parmesan cheese if desired.

# Tagliatelle Carbonara

*SERVES 4*

*Bacon, cream and eggs combine to make a rich pasta sauce.*

PREPARATION: 10 mins
COOKING: 15 mins

---

300g/10oz tagliatelle
30g/1oz butter or margarine
120g/4oz streaky bacon rashers, chopped
1 tbsp olive oil
4 tbsps single cream
Pinch of paprika
60g/2oz Parmesan cheese, grated
2 eggs
Salt and pepper

---

**Step 4** Beat together eggs and grated cheese.

**Step 7** Add bacon mixture and egg mixture, and toss together.

**1.** Heat the oil in a frying pan, and cook the bacon over a moderate heat until just browning.

**2.** Add the paprika and cook for 1 minute.

**3.** Add the cream, and stir.

**4.** Beat together the eggs and grated cheese.

**5.** Cook the tagliatelle in lots of boiling salted water for 10 minutes, or until tender but still firm.

**6.** Drain the pasta, return to pan with butter and black pepper, and toss.

**7.** Add bacon mixture and egg mixture, and toss together. Add salt to taste. Serve immediately.

# Spaghetti with Tomato, Salami and Green Olives

## SERVES 4

*This robust pasta dish is ideal for a quick supper or light lunch.*

PREPARATION: 15 mins
COOKING: 15 mins

300g/10oz spaghetti
400g/14oz tin plum tomatoes
150g/5oz salami, sliced
200g/7oz green olives, stoned and chopped
1 clove garlic, crushed
2 tbsps olive oil
½ tbsp oregano
60g/2oz pecorino cheese, grated
Salt and pepper

**Step 1** Purée tomatoes and push through a sieve into a saucepan.

**Step 2** Add oregano, salami and olives and heat gently.

**1.** Purée tomatoes, and push through a sieve into a saucepan.

**2.** Add oregano, salami and olives, and heat gently.

**3.** Add salt and pepper to taste.

**4.** Meanwhile, cook spaghetti in plenty of boiling salted water for 10 minutes. Drain well.

**5.** Heat olive oil, garlic and freshly-ground black pepper in the pan used to cook the spaghetti.

**6.** Add spaghetti, and pour the sauce over. Toss well and serve immediately with pecorino cheese.

# Pasta with Fresh Tomato and Basil Sauce

*SERVES 4*

*Fresh tomato and basil make a classic sauce for pasta.*

PREPARATION: 15-20 mins
COOKING: 10-15 mins

1 small onion, finely chopped
450g/1lb fresh tomatoes
2 tbsps tomato purée
1 orange
2 cloves garlic, crushed
Salt and freshly ground black pepper
140ml/¼ pint red wine
140ml/¼ pint chicken stock
2 tbsps coarsely chopped basil
340g/12oz wholemeal pasta

1. Peel and finely chop the onion.

2. Cut a small cross in the skins of the tomatoes and plunge them into boiling water for 30 seconds. Remove and carefully peel away the loosened skin.

3. Cut the tomatoes into quarters, and remove and discard the pips. Chop the tomato flesh roughly, and put this, the onion and the tomato purée into a large saucepan.

4. Heat the onion and tomatoes over a gentle heat, stirring continuously until the tomatoes soften and begin to lose their juice.

**Step 1** To chop an onion finely, pierce the peeled onion with a fork and use this to hold the vegetable steady whilst you chop.

5. Finely grate the rind from the orange. Cut the orange in half and squeeze out the juice.

6. Put the orange rind and juice into a large saucepan along with all the remaining ingredients, and bring to the boil.

7. Continue to boil until the sauce has reduced and thickened and the vegetables are soft.

8. Whilst the sauce is cooking, put the pasta into another saucepan with enough boiling water to cover. Season with a little salt and cook for 10-15 minutes, or until the pasta is soft.

9. Drain the pasta in a colander, and stir it into the hot sauce. Serve at once with a salad.

# Tagliatelle with Garlic and Oil

## SERVES 4

*Garlic and oil combine to make the simplest of pasta sauces.*

PREPARATION: 5 mins
COOKING: 10 mins

300g/10oz green tagliatelle
150ml/¼ pint olive oil
3 cloves garlic, crushed
2 tbsps chopped parsley
Salt and pepper

**Step 5** Toss the tagliatelle in the sauce to coat well.

**Step 5** Add sauce to tagliatelle.

**1.** Cook the tagliatelle in lots of boiling salted water for 10 minutes, or until tender but still firm, stirring occasionally.

**2.** Meanwhile, heat the oil in a pan and, when warm, add peeled, crushed garlic.

**3.** Fry gently until golden brown.

**4.** Add chopped parsley, and salt and pepper to taste.

**5.** Drain tagliatelle. Add sauce, and toss to coat well. Serve hot.

# Home-made Tagliatelle with Summer Sauce

*SERVES 4*

*Home-made pasta is in a class by itself.*

PREPARATION: 30 mins
COOKING: 5-6 mins

*Pasta Dough*
120g/4oz plain flour
120g/4oz fine semolina
2 large eggs
2 tsps olive oil
Pinch salt

*Sauce*
450g/1lb unpeeled tomatoes, seeded and cut
    into small dice
1 large green pepper, cored, seeded and cut in
    small dice
1 onion, cut in small dice
1 tbsp chopped fresh basil
1 tbsp chopped fresh parsley
2 cloves garlic, crushed
140ml/¼ pint olive oil and vegetable oil mixed

**1.** Place the flours in a mound on a work
surface and make a well in the centre. Place the
eggs, oil and salt in the centre of the well.

**2.** Using a fork, beat the ingredients in the
centre to blend them and gradually incorporate
the flour from the outside edge.

**3.** When half the flour is incorporated, start
kneading using the palms of the hands and not

**Step 4** Roll the dough out thinly and cut into thin strips.

the fingers. Cover the dough and leave it to rest
for 15 minutes.

**4.** Divide the dough in quarters and roll out
thinly with a rolling pin on a floured surface or
use a pasta machine, dusting dough lightly with
flour before rolling. Allow the sheets of pasta to
dry for about 10 minutes on a floured surface.
Cut the sheets into strips about 5mm/¼ inch
wide by hand or machine, dusting lightly with
flour while cutting. Leave the cut pasta to dry
while preparing the sauce.

**5.** Combine all the sauce ingredients, mixing
well. Cover and refrigerate.

**6.** Cook the pasta for 5-6 minutes in boiling
salted water with a spoonful of oil. Drain the
pasta and rinse under very hot water. Toss in a
colander to drain excess water. Place in a
serving dish and pour the cold sauce over.

# Penne with Ham and Asparagus

## SERVES 4

*The Italian word penne means quills, due to the diagonal cut on both ends.*

PREPARATION: 20 mins
COOKING: 10 mins

225g/8oz penne
340g/12oz fresh asparagus
120g/4oz cooked ham
30g/2 tbsps butter or margarine
280ml/½ pint double cream

**1.** Using a swivel vegetable peeler, scrape the sides of the asparagus spears starting about 5cm/2 inches from the top. Cut off the ends of the spears about 2.5cm/1 inch from the bottom.

**2.** Cut the ham into strips about 1.25cm/½ inch thick.

**3.** Bring a sauté pan of salted water to the boil. Move the pan so it is half on and half off direct

**Step 1** Peel the asparagus stalks with a swivel vegetable peeler.

**Step 4** Cut ham and cooked asparagus into 2.5cm/1 inch lengths. Leave the asparagus tips whole.

heat. Place in the asparagus spears so that the tips are off the heat. Cover and bring back to the boil. Cook the asparagus spears for about 2 minutes. Drain and allow to cool.

**4.** Cut the asparagus into 5cm/1 inch lengths, leaving the tips whole.

**5.** Melt the butter in the sauté pan and add the asparagus and ham. Cook briefly to evaporate the liquid, and add the cream. Bring to the boil and cook for about 5 minutes to thicken the cream.

**6.** Meanwhile, cook the pasta in boiling salted water with a little oil for about 10-12 minutes.

**7.** Drain the pasta and rinse under hot water. Toss in a colander to drain and mix with the sauce. Serve with grated Parmesan cheese, if desired.

# Spaghetti Amatriciana

## SERVES 4

*Chilli pepper brings a fiery taste to this pasta sauce.*

PREPARATION: 20-25 mins
COOKING: 10-12 mins

1 onion
6 strips smoked bacon
450g/1lb ripe tomatoes
1 red chilli pepper
1½ tbsps oil
340g/12oz spaghetti

**1.** Slice the onion thinly. Remove rind from the bacon and cut into thin strips.

**2.** Drop the tomatoes into boiling water for 6-8 seconds. Remove and place in cold water, and leave to cool. This will make the peels easier to remove.

**3.** When the tomatoes are peeled, cut them in half and remove the seeds and pulp with a

**Step 2** Placing tomatoes in boiling water and then in cold water makes the skins easier to remove.

**Step 4** Remove the stems, seeds and cores from the chilli pepper, cut into thin strips and then chop into fine dice.

teaspoon. Chop the tomato flesh roughly and set it aside.

**4.** Cut the chilli pepper in half lengthways. Remove the seeds and core and cut the pepper into thin strips. Cut the strips into small dice.

**5.** Heat the oil in a sauté pan and add the onion and bacon. Stir over medium heat for about 5 minutes, until the onion is transparent. Drain off excess fat and add the tomatoes and chilli and mix well. Simmer the sauce gently, uncovered, for about 5 minutes, stirring occasionally.

**6.** Meanwhile, cook the spaghetti in boiling salted water with a little oil for about 10-12 minutes. Drain and rinse in hot water and toss in a colander to dry. To serve, spoon the sauce on top of the spaghetti and sprinkle with freshly grated Parmesan cheese.

# Spirali with Spinach and Bacon

## SERVES 4

*Pasta doesn't have to have a sauce that cooks for hours.*
*This whole dish takes about 20 minutes. True Italian "fast food"!*

PREPARATION: 10 mins
COOKING: 10 mins

---

340g/12oz pasta spirals
225g/8oz fresh spinach
90g/3oz bacon
1 clove garlic, crushed
1 small red or green chilli pepper
1 small red sweet pepper
1 small onion
3 tbsps olive oil
Salt and pepper

---

**1.** Cook the pasta in boiling salted water for about 10-12 minutes or until just tender. Drain in a colander and rinse. Keep the pasta in a bowl of water until ready to use.

**Step 2** Tear stalks off the spinach and wash the leaves well.

**Step 4** Roll up the leaves in several layers to shred them faster.

**2.** Tear the stalks off the spinach and wash the leaves well, changing the water several times. Set aside to drain.

**3.** Remove the rind from the bacon and dice the bacon finely. Cut the chilli and the red pepper in half, remove the stems, core and seeds and slice finely. Slice the onion thinly.

**4.** Shred the spinach finely.

**5.** Heat the oil in a sauté pan and add garlic, onion, peppers and bacon. Fry for 2 minutes, add the spinach and fry for a further 2 minutes, stirring continuously. Season with salt and pepper.

**6.** Drain the pasta spirals and toss them in a colander to remove excess water. Mix with the spinach sauce and serve immediately.

# Gianfottere Salad

*SERVES 4*

*This delicious Italian salad makes the most of summer vegetables.*

PREPARATION: 30 mins
COOKING: 30 mins

1 small aubergine
2 tomatoes
1 large courgette
1 red pepper
1 green pepper
1 medium onion
1 clove garlic, peeled
4 tbsps olive oil
Salt and pepper
450g/1lb wholemeal pasta spirals

**1.** Cut the aubergine into 1cm/½-inch slices. Sprinkle with salt and leave for 30 minutes.

**2.** Chop the tomatoes roughly and remove the cores.

**3.** Cut the courgette into 1cm/½-inch slices.

**Step 1** Cut the aubergine into 1cm/½-inch slices and sprinkle with plenty of salt.

**Step 8** Add the aubergine, courgette, peppers, tomatoes and garlic to the onion in the frying pan.

**4.** Core and seed the peppers, and chop them roughly.

**5.** Chop the onion. Crush the garlic.

**6.** Heat 3 tbsps olive oil in a frying pan, and fry the onion gently, until it is transparent.

**7.** Rinse the salt from the aubergine and pat dry. Chop the aubergine roughly.

**8.** Stir the aubergine, courgette, peppers, tomatoes and garlic into the onion, and fry gently for 20 minutes. Season to taste, and allow to cool completely.

**9.** Cook the pasta spirals in plenty of boiling salted water for 10-15 minutes.

**10.** Rinse the pasta in cold water and drain well.

**11.** Put the pasta into a large mixing bowl, and stir in the remaining olive oil.

**12.** Stir in the vegetables, mixing well.

# Tuna and Tomato Salad

*SERVES 4*

*Serve this salad as part of a summer lunch with a green salad and French bread.*

PREPARATION: 10 mins
COOKING: 15 mins

1 tbsp chopped fresh basil, or marjoram
6 tbsps French dressing
340g/12oz pasta spirals
6 tomatoes
340g/12oz tinned tuna fish, drained

**1.** Mix the basil or marjoram, with the French dressing.

**2.** Cook the pasta in a large saucepan of boiling, lightly salted water, for about 10 minutes.

**3.** Rinse in cold water and drain well, shaking off any excess water.

**4.** Put the pasta into a large bowl and toss with

**Step 4** Mix the pasta spirals with 3 tbsps of the French dressing in a large bowl.

**Step 7** Add the tuna to the pasta and mix together gently.

3 tablespoons of the French dressing, mixing well to ensure that they are evenly coated. Leave to cool.

**5.** Slice enough of the tomatoes to arrange around the outside of the serving dish and then chop the rest.

**6.** Put the chopped tomatoes into another bowl and pour over the remaining French dressing. Put this into the centre of a serving dish.

**7.** Add the flaked tuna to the pasta and toss together gently.

**8.** Pile the pasta and tuna over the chopped tomatoes in the centre of the dish.

**9.** Arrange the tomato slices around the edge of the serving dish and chill well until required.

# Mushroom Pasta Salad

### SERVES 4

*The piquant lemon marinade brings zest to this easy salad.*

PREPARATION: 10 mins, plus 1 hr to marinate the mushrooms
COOKING: 15 mins

---

5 tbsps olive oil
Juice of 2 lemons
1 tsp fresh chopped basil
1 tsp fresh chopped parsley
Salt and pepper
225g/8oz mushrooms
225g/8oz wholemeal pasta shapes

---

**1.** Mix together the olive oil, lemon juice, herbs and seasoning.

**Step 2** Use a sharp knife to slice the mushrooms thinly.

**Step 6** Stir the cooled pasta into the marinated mushrooms, mixing well to coat evenly.

**2.** Finely slice the mushrooms and add these to the lemon dressing in the bowl, stirring well.

**3.** Cover the bowl and allow to stand in a cool place for at least 1 hour.

**4.** Cook the pasta in boiling, salted water for 10-15 minutes.

**5.** Rinse the pasta in cold water and drain well.

**6.** Add the pasta to the marinated mushrooms and lemon dressing, mixing well to coat evenly.

**7.** Adjust the seasoning if necessary, then chill well before serving.

# Macaroni Cheese with Frankfurters

### SERVES 4

*A hearty family supper dish, ideal for cold winter evenings.*

PREPARATION: 10 mins
COOKING: 20 mins

8 frankfurter sausages
450g/1lb macaroni
60g/2oz butter or margarine
90g/3oz plain flour
560ml/1 pint milk
180g/6oz Cheddar cheese, grated
1 tsp dry mustard powder
Salt and pepper

**1.** Poach the frankfurters for 5-6 minutes in slightly salted boiling water.

**2.** Remove the skins from the frankfurters and, when cold, slice the meat diagonally.

**3.** Cook the macaroni in plenty of boiling salted water for about 10-15 minutes.

**Step 2** Remove the skins from the frankfurters and cut them diagonally into slices about 2.5cm/1 inch long.

**Step 6** Add the milk gradually, beating the mixture well between additions, until all the milk is incorporated.

**4.** Rinse in cold water and drain well.

**5.** Melt the butter in a saucepan. Stir in the flour and cook for 1 minute.

**6.** Remove the pan from the heat and add the milk gradually, beating thoroughly and returning the pan to the heat to cook between additions. When all the milk has been added, simmer for 2 minutes, stirring occasionally.

**7.** Stir in the frankfurters, grated cheese and mustard. Season to taste.

**8.** Add the drained macaroni to the sauce and stir well until heated through.

**9.** Pour the mixture into an ovenproof dish and sprinkle the top with a little extra grated cheese.

**10.** Cook under a preheated moderate grill, until the top is golden brown.

# Lasagne Rolls

*SERVES 4*

*An interesting way of using sheets of lasagne.*

PREPARATION: 10 mins
COOKING: 15 mins

8 lasagne sheets
60g/2oz button mushrooms, sliced
225g/8oz boned chicken breast
30g/1oz butter, or margarine
30g/1oz plain flour
140ml/¼ pint milk
          Gruyère or Cheddar cheese, grated
Salt and pepper

**1.** Fill a large saucepan two thirds full with salted water. Add a little oil and bring to the boil.

**2.** Add 1 sheet of lasagne, wait about 2 minutes, then add another sheet. Cook only a few at a time and after about 6-7 minutes, remove and rinse under cold water. Allow to drain.

**3.** Repeat this process until all the lasagne is cooked.

**4.** Wash and slice the mushrooms, and slice the chicken breast into thin strips.

**5.** Melt half the butter in a small frying pan and fry the mushrooms and the chicken.

**6.** In a small saucepan, melt the rest of the butter. Stir in the flour and cook for 1 minute.

**Step 11** Spread the chicken mixture evenly over each sheet of lasagne and roll up like a swiss roll.

**7.** Remove the pan from the heat and add the milk gradually, stirring well and returning the pan to the heat between additions, to thicken the sauce.

**8.** Beat the sauce well and cook for 3 minutes.

**9.** Pour the sauce into the frying pan with the chicken and the mushrooms. Add half the cheese and mix well. Season to taste.

**10.** Lay the sheets of lasagne on a board and divide the chicken mixture equally between them.

**11.** Spread the chicken mixture evenly over each lasagne sheet and roll up lengthways, like a swiss roll.

**12.** Put the rolls into an ovenproof dish. Sprinkle with the remaining cheese and grill under a pre-heated moderate grill, until the cheese is bubbly and golden brown.

# *Lasagne Napoletana*

### SERVES 6

*This is lasagne as it is cooked and eaten in Naples.*

PREPARATION: 25 mins
COOKING: 1-1¼hrs

9 sheets spinach lasagne

*Tomato Sauce*
3 tbsps olive oil
2 cloves garlic, crushed
900g/2lbs tinned tomatoes, drained
2 tbsps chopped fresh basil, six whole leaves
   reserved
Salt and pepper
Pinch sugar

*Cheese Filling*
450g/1lb ricotta cheese
60g/2oz unsalted butter
225g/8oz Mozzarella cheese, grated
Salt and pepper
Pinch nutmeg

**1.** Cook the pasta for 8 minutes in boiling salted water with a little oil. Drain and rinse under hot water and place in a single layer on a damp cloth. Cover with another damp cloth and set aside.

**2.** To prepare the sauce, cook the garlic in remaining oil for about 1 minute in a large saucepan. When pale brown, add the tomatoes, basil, salt, pepper and sugar.

**Step 5**
Carefully spread the softened cheese mixture on top of the tomato sauce.

**3.** Lower the heat under the saucepan and simmer the sauce for 35 minutes. Add more seasoning or sugar to taste.

**4.** Beat the ricotta cheese and butter together until creamy and stir into the remaining ingredients.

**5.** Place 3 sheets of lasagne on the base of a greased baking dish. Cover with one third of the sauce and carefully spread on a layer of cheese. Place another 3 layers of pasta over the cheese and cover with another third of the sauce. Add the remaining cheese filling and cover with the remaining pasta. Spoon the remaining sauce on top.

**6.** Cover with foil and bake for 20 minutes at 190°/375°F/Gas Mark 5. Uncover and cook for 10 minutes longer. Garnish with the reserved leaves and leave to stand 10-15 minutes before serving.

# Fish Ravioli

### SERVES 4

*This ravioli dish is served with a subtly flavoured cream and lemon sauce.*

PREPARATION: 30 mins
COOKING: 30 mins

*Dough*
275g/9oz strong plain flour
3 eggs

225g/8oz sole fillets
2 tbsps breadcrumbs
2 eggs, beaten
1 spring onion, finely chopped
1 slice of onion
1 slice of lemon
6 peppercorns
1 bay leaf
1 tbsp lemon juice
300ml/½ pint water

*Lemon sauce*
30g/1oz butter or margarine
30g/1oz flour
2 tbsps double cream
2 tbsps lemon juice

**Step 6** Shape the filling into small balls, and set them about 4cm/1½" apart on one half of the dough.

breadcrumbs and spring onion, and season.

**4.** Sift flour into a bowl and add the eggs. Work together with a spoon, then knead by hand, until smooth. Leave for 15 minutes.

**5.** Lightly flour a board, and roll out dough thinly into a rectangle. Cut dough in half.

**6.** Shape the filling into small balls, and set them about 4cm/1½" apart on one half of the dough. Place the other half on top, and cut with a ravioli cutter. Seal the edges.

**7.** Cook in batches in boiling salted water for about 8 minutes, then drain.

**1.** Pre-heat oven to 180°C/350°F/Gas Mark 4. Place fish in oven-proof dish with onion, lemon, peppercorns, bay leaf, lemon juice and water. Cover and cook for 20 minutes.

**2.** Remove fish from liquid, and allow to drain. Strain liquid, and set aside.

**3.** When fish is cool, beat to a pulp. Add 2 eggs,

**8.** To make sauce, melt butter in a pan, then stir in flour. Draw off heat, and gradually stir in liquid from cooked fish. Return to heat and bring to boil. Simmer, add cream and mix well. Season.

**9.** Remove from heat, and gradually stir in lemon juice. Do not reboil. Pour sauce over ravioli and serve.

# Cannelloni

*SERVES 4*

*This tasty meat dish justifiably remains a favourite.*

PREPARATION: 10 mins
COOKING: 1 hr

12 cannelloni shells
2 tbsps Parmesan cheese, grated

450g/1lb minced beef
1 tbsp olive oil
1 onion, peeled and chopped
2 cloves garlic, crushed
225g/8oz packet frozen spinach, thawed
½ tsp oregano
1 tsp tomato purée
4 tbsps cream
1 egg, lightly beaten

*Tomato sauce*
1 tbsp olive oil
1 onion, peeled and chopped
1 clove garlic, crushed
400g/14oz tin plum tomatoes
2 tbsps tomato purée

*Béchamel sauce*
300ml/½ pint milk
30g/1oz butter or margarine
30g/1oz flour

**1.** Heat the oil in a pan, and fry garlic and onion gently until soft and transparent.

**2.** Add meat and cook until well browned. Add

**Step 4**
Carefully fill the cannelloni with the meat mixture.

tomato purée, and oregano, and cook gently for 15 minutes.

**3.** Add spinach, egg and cream, and salt and pepper to taste.

**4.** Cook pasta in boiling salted water for 15-20 minutes. Rinse and drain. Fill with meat mixture.

**5.** To make the tomato sauce, heat the oil in a pan, add onion and garlic, and cook gently until transparent. Add tomatoes, tomato purée and season to taste. Bring to boil, and then simmer for 5 minutes. Set aside.

**6.** To make the Béchamel sauce, melt butter in pan. Remove from heat and stir in flour. Gradually add milk, and bring to boil, stirring continuously, until sauce thickens. Add seasoning.

**7.** Spread tomato sauce in an oven-proof dish. Lay pasta on top, and cover with Béchamel sauce. Sprinkle with Parmesan cheese, and bake at 180°C/350°F/Gas Mark 4 for 30 minutes.

# Spinach Lasagne

*SERVES 4*

*Spinach flavoured with nutmeg makes a delicious filling for lasagne.*

PREPARATION: 10 mins
COOKING: 30 mins

8 sheets green lasagne

*Spinach sauce*
90g/3oz butter or margarine
325g/11oz packet of frozen spinach, thawed
  and chopped finely
Pinch of ground nutmeg
90g/3oz flour
150ml/¼ pint milk
Salt and pepper

*Mornay sauce*
30g/1oz butter or margarine
30g/1oz flour
300ml/½ pint milk
90g/3oz Parmesan cheese, grated
1 tsp French mustard
Salt

**1.** To make spinach sauce, heat butter in pan, stir in flour and cook for 30 seconds.

**2.** Draw off heat and stir in milk gradually.

**3.** Return to heat, and bring to the boil, stirring continuously. Cook for 3 minutes.

**4.** Add spinach, nutmeg, and salt and pepper to taste. Set aside.

**Step 9** Line the base with a layer of lasagne, followed by some of the spinach mixture and a layer of cheese sauce.

**5.** Cook spinach lasagne in lots of boiling salted water for 10 minutes. Rinse in cold water and drain carefully. Dry on a clean cloth.

**6.** To make Mornay sauce, heat butter in pan and stir in flour, cooking for 30 seconds.

**7.** Remove from heat, and stir in milk. Return to heat, stirring continuously, until boiling. Continue stirring, and simmer for 3 minutes.

**8.** Draw off heat, and add mustard and two-thirds of cheese, and salt to taste.

**9.** Grease an oven-proof baking dish. Line the base with a layer of lasagne, followed by some of the spinach mixture, and a layer of cheese sauce.

**10.** Repeat the process finishing with a layer of lasagne with a covering of cheese sauce.

**11.** Sprinkle with the remaining cheese. Bake in a hot oven 200°C/400°F/Gas Mark 7 until golden on top. Serve immediately.

# Index

Spaghetti with Tomato, Salami and Green Olives